Ladders

Rainforest Animals

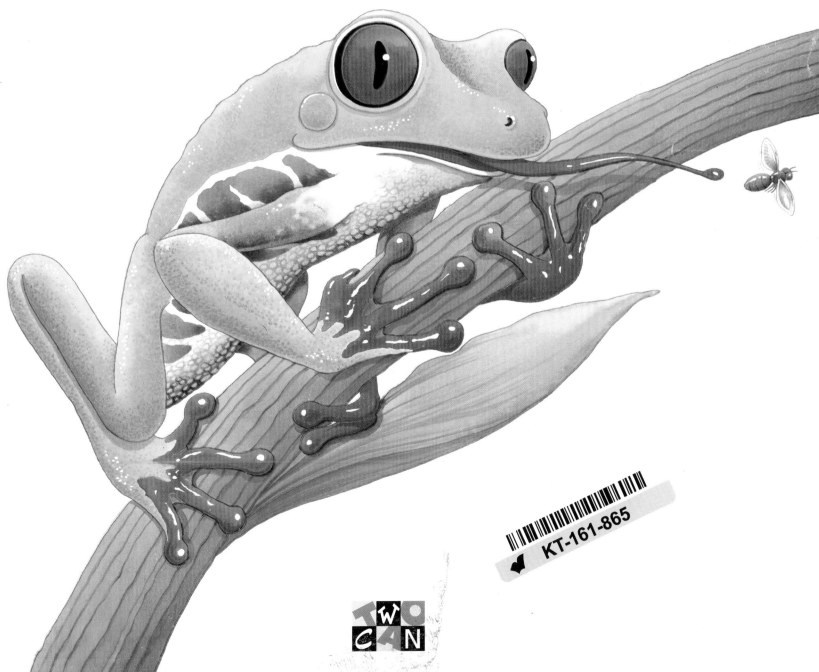

TWO CAN

Created and published by
Two-Can Publishing Ltd
346 Old Street
London
EC1V 9RB

Written by: Angela Wilkes
Story by: Belinda Webster
Consultant: Dr Sandra Knapp, Natural History Museum, London
Main illustrations: Steve Holmes
Computer illustrations: Jon Stuart
Editors: Sarah Levete and Julia Hillyard
Designers: Lisa Nutt and Alex Frampton
Managing editor: Deborah Kespert
Art director: Belinda Webster
Production manager: Adam Wilde
Picture researchers: Jenny West and Liz Eddison

First published by Two-Can Publishing Ltd in 1999

Hardback ISBN 1 85434 534 6
Paperback ISBN 1 85434 535 4

Dewey Decimal Classification 591.5

Hardback 10 9 8 7 6 5 4 3 2 1
Paperback 10 9 8 7 6 5 4 3 2 1

A catalogue record for this book is available from the British Library.

Photographic credits: p4: Planet Earth Pictures; p6: Bruce Coleman Ltd; p7: Oxford Scientific Films;
p8: Tony Stone Images; p9: Bruce Coleman Ltd; p11: Planet Earth Pictures; p14: Oxford Scientific Films;
p15: Bruce Coleman Ltd; p16: Oxford Scientific Films; p17: Bruce Coleman Ltd; p18: Oxford Scientific Films;
p21: Bruce Coleman Ltd; p22: Oxford Scientific Films.

Printed in Hong Kong by Wing King Tong

What's inside?

This book tells you about lots of exciting animals that live in the hot and steamy rainforests of South America. Some of the animals swing or fly through the tree-tops, others make their homes on the forest floor.

Monkey

Monkeys live in groups in the trees. They are amazing acrobats that leap from branch to branch and swing from the dangling vines. When monkeys play, they screech and whoop loudly. What a racket!

A monkey holds on to the branches with its strong **arms**. ....

Monkeys **chat** and squabble with each other. They also pull funny faces.

A golden lion tamarin monkey has a shaggy golden coat. The fur around its face is so thick, you can't see its ears!

It's a fact!

Howler monkeys are the noisiest animals in the rainforest. You can hear their deafening howls from miles away!

To keep steady, a monkey curls its long **tail** tightly around the branches.

Sharp **eyesight** helps a monkey to spot danger and to stay safe.

Hands, that can grasp like yours, are perfect for picking fruit.

Sloth

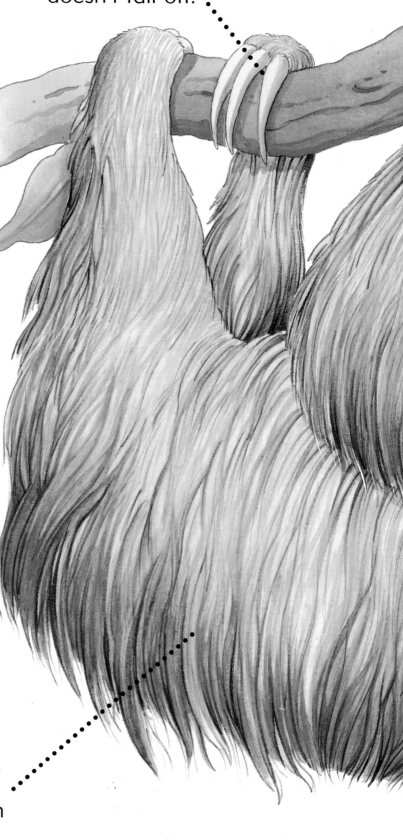

A sloth spends most of its life hanging upside down, fast asleep. When this strange-looking creature wakes up, it crawls along its branch, looking for leaves to eat. About once a week, it creeps slowly down the tree trunk to explore the ground.

A sloth crawls along the forest floor. It takes half an hour to move as far as you can walk in one minute!

A sloth hooks its three **claws** tightly over a branch, so that it doesn't fall off.

Shaggy **hair** grows down from a sloth's belly. This helps rain to run off easily.

A **baby sloth** clings on to its mother's belly where it is cosy and safe.

A sloth hardly ever washes! Green **slime** grows on its hair.

A sloth sleeps for up to 18 hours a day. It doesn't need to eat much food because it is hardly ever awake.

Bat

When night falls, bats wake up. They stretch their wings and leave their daytime resting places in trees and caves. Bats have sharp hearing and excellent eyesight to help them find their way around in the dark.

A bat goes to sleep hanging upside down. It folds its leathery wings neatly across its furry body to stay warm.

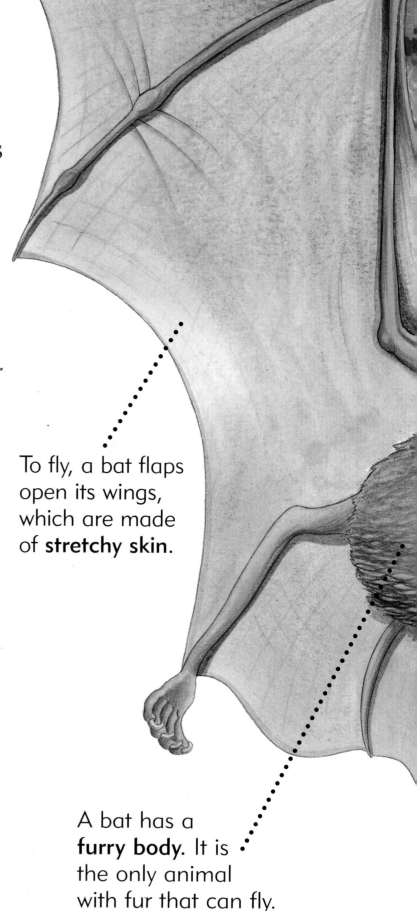

To fly, a bat flaps open its wings, which are made of **stretchy skin**.

A bat has a **furry body**. It is the only animal with fur that can fly.

This bat's large **ears** pick up sounds that even you cannot hear.

These baby tent bats snuggle up in a palm leaf. They will stay here until they are big enough to fly away.

A big **nose** sniffs out the ripest fruit and tastiest insects to eat.

Sharp **teeth** help this bat to chew juicy pieces of fruit.

# Colourful birds

High up, in the leafy tree-tops, hundreds of rainbow-coloured birds sing and squawk. They swoop through the trees looking for fruit and nuts. You may even spot a macaw, one of the biggest birds in the rainforest, munching a tasty treat.

Colourful **markings** help macaws to spot each other among the leaves.

It's a fact!

Hummingbirds are the smallest birds in the world. One kind is so tiny that it can perch on the tip of a pencil!

A macaw's waterproof **feathers** are similar to a raincoat. They keep out the pouring rain.

It's easy to soar through the trees with powerful **wings**.

A strong, hooked **beak** is perfect for cracking open tough nuts to eat.

Sharp, curly claws, called **talons**, help a macaw to grip branches or hold nuts.

A toucan's giant beak looks heavy but it is hollow and light. It's made from the same material as your fingernails.

In the tree-tops

The tree-tops are packed with noisy animals playing and looking for food. Look at how they leap, climb and fly!

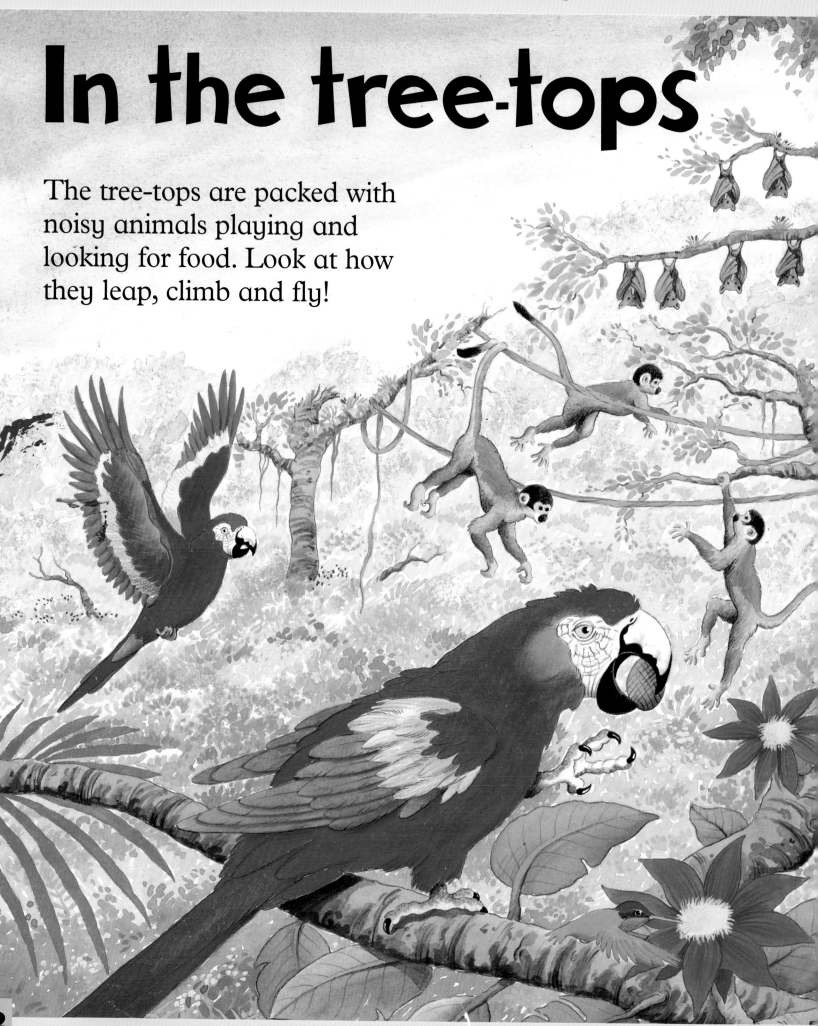

How many tiny hummingbirds are flying around the flowers?

Which animal has green slime on its long, shaggy fur?

How do the furry monkeys swing from tree to tree?

Which group of animals is hanging upside down fast asleep?

Words you know

Here are some words that you learned earlier. Say them out loud, then try to find the things in the picture.

beak   claws   furry body
wings   tail   feathers

13

What is the bright macaw doing with its sharp beak?

Frog

A frog breathes through its **slimy skin**, as well as through its nose.

All kinds of brightly coloured frogs leap around the steamy forest floor. They splash in rivers and make their homes in puddles left by the rain. The red-eyed tree frog in the big picture is an expert at climbing trees.

Strong back **legs** are useful for hopping after insects or springing away from enemies.

Two poison-arrow frogs crouch on a leaf. Their bright patterns warn hungry enemies that they are deadly poisonous.

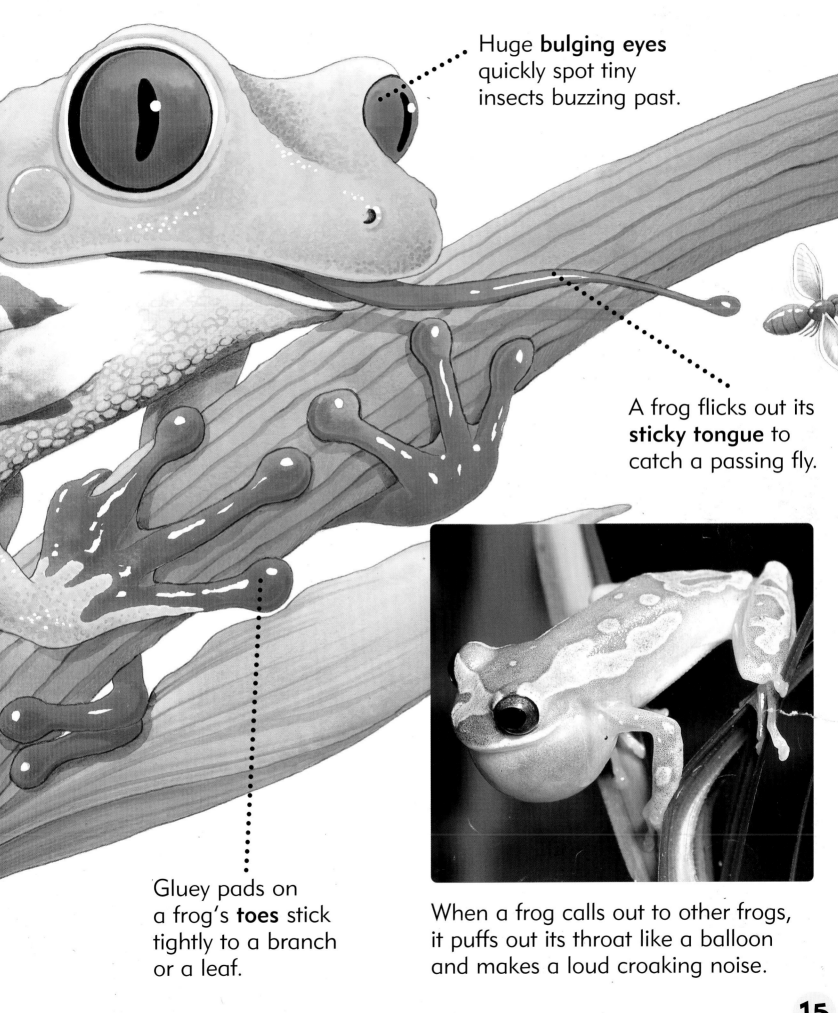

Huge **bulging eyes** quickly spot tiny insects buzzing past.

A frog flicks out its **sticky tongue** to catch a passing fly.

Gluey pads on a frog's **toes** stick tightly to a branch or a leaf.

When a frog calls out to other frogs, it puffs out its throat like a balloon and makes a loud croaking noise.

Jaguar

A jaguar is a fierce hunter. At night, it prowls between the tree trunks, then lies in wait for animals to kill and eat. It can climb up trees and even swim after crocodiles. The jaguar is the biggest and most powerful cat in the rainforest. Watch out!

Long **whiskers** help a jaguar to feel its way through the thick grass.

Playing is a fun way for a young **cub** to learn how to fight and hunt.

A hungry jaguar creeps up on a small animal. Suddenly, the jaguar pounces before the animal has time to escape.

A jaguar has sharp **eyesight**. It can even see in the dark.

It's comfortable up here! A tree is a perfect place to lie in wait for a tasty meal or take an afternoon nap.

A spotty **coat** makes a jaguar hard to see among the shady trees.

Soft padded **paws** hide dangerous sharp claws.

Snake

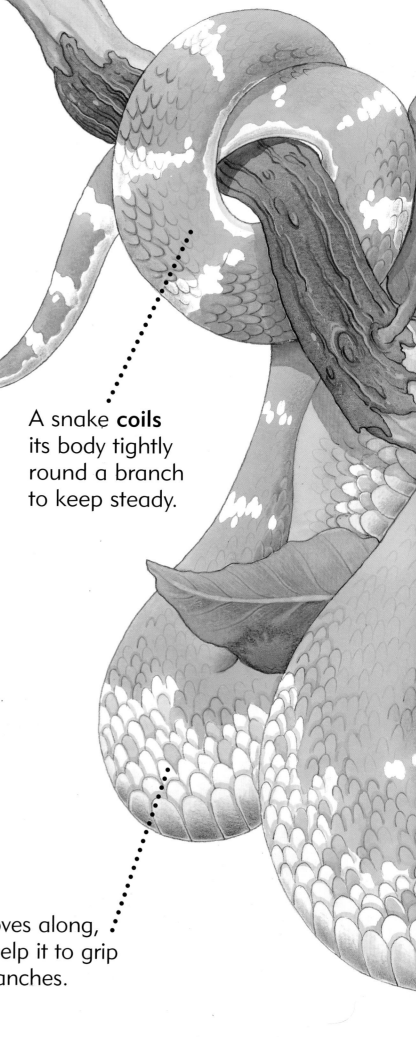

Snakes slither across the dark forest floor and climb up trees. The emerald tree boa in the big picture is hanging silently from a branch, ready to pounce on a tasty frog snack. After a really big meal, it may not eat again for a whole year!

A snake **coils** its body tightly round a branch to keep steady.

This viper is about to attack. It will dart forwards, then sink its poisonous teeth, called fangs, into its enemy.

As a snake moves along, rough **scales** help it to grip the slippery branches.

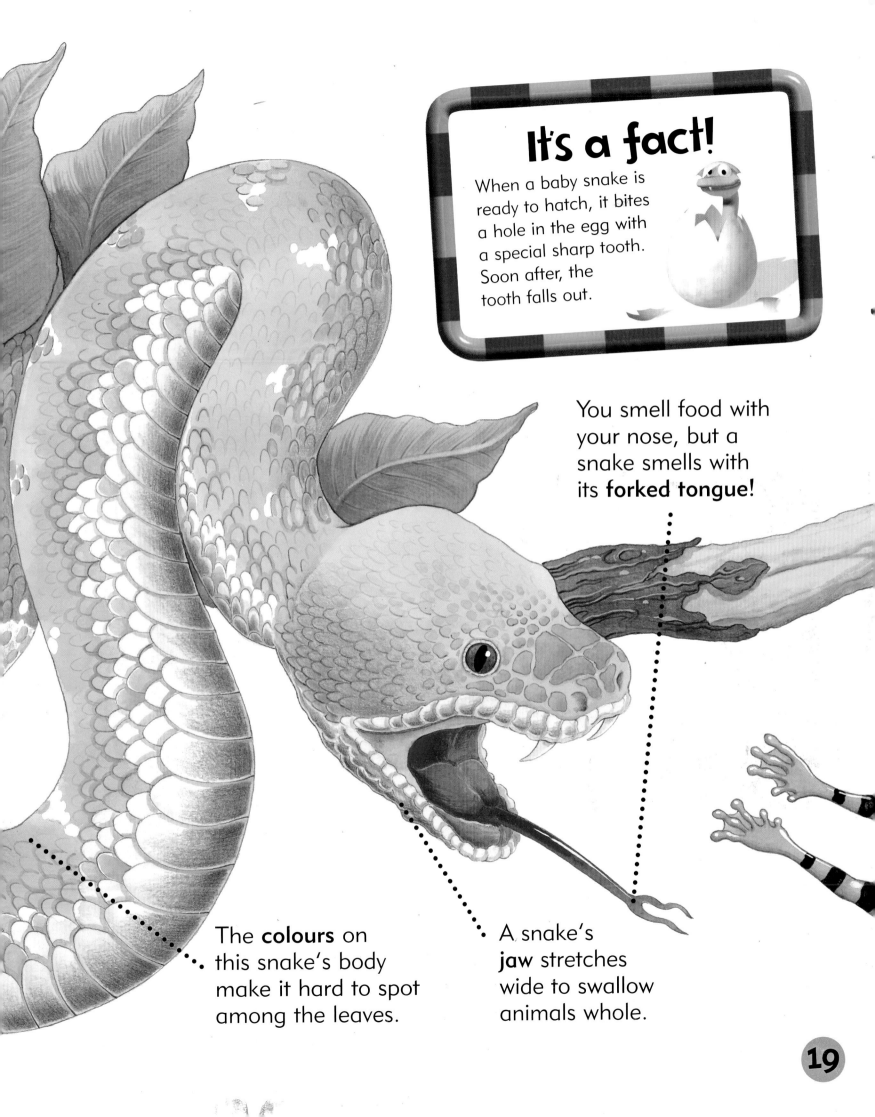

It's a fact!

When a baby snake is ready to hatch, it bites a hole in the egg with a special sharp tooth. Soon after, the tooth falls out.

You smell food with your nose, but a snake smells with its **forked tongue!**

The **colours** on this snake's body make it hard to spot among the leaves.

A snake's **jaw** stretches wide to swallow animals whole.

19

 # Crocodile

A crocodile spends the day lying lazily in the warm sunshine. In the evening, it floats silently in a cool river, keeping its eyes just above the water, on the lookout for its next meal.

It's a fact!

A baby crocodile is born on land. Its mother gently picks it up in her mouth and carries it safely to the river's edge.

When a crocodile dives, its **nostrils** shut tight to stop water flowing in.

Wide **jaws** are perfect for snapping up tasty fish and even large animals.

A crocodile's **teeth** are sharp enough to cut a piece of wood in half!

Tough scaly skin, called a **hide**, protects a crocodile's back.

A crocodile waddles along the ground on short, **stocky legs**.

Paddling through the water is easy with **webbed feet**.

This crafty crocodile looks like a floating log, covered in weeds. But watch out – with one swish of its tail, it will pounce!

Creepy crawlies

More kinds of creepy crawlies live in the rainforest than anywhere else in the world. They include hard-working ants, beautiful butterflies and giant spiders. These creatures have clever ways of finding food and hiding from enemies.

A **leafcutter ant** carries leaves back to its nest to make food.

This shiny yellow beetle hides among the leaves of plants, or burrows into woody stems, where it is safe from attackers.

A hard **case** protects the ant's body like a tough coat of armour.

A **butterfly** lands next to a flower to drink the sweet juice inside.

A special long **tongue**, shaped like a straw, sucks up the juice.

Hundreds of tiny scales make up the bright **patterns** on a butterfly's wings.

An ant smells, tastes and touches the world around it with **feelers**.

It's a fact!

A bird-eating spider can be as big as a dinner plate!

23

The forest floor

On the dark, damp forest floor, all kinds of animals are busy hunting, playing and looking after their families.

24

Words you know

Here are some words that you learned earlier. Say them out loud, then try to find the things in the picture.

paws   jaguar cub   feelers
coat   webbed feet   snout

How many ants are crawling along the log?

Where is the red and yellow butterfly resting?

25

Message to the tree-tops

Pitter, patter, splat. Pitter, patter, splat.
Frog woke up to berries landing on her head.
What a mess. Squashed berries everywhere.

"Not again," Frog muttered, looking up into the trees towering above her.

Someone must be dropping them on purpose. "Hey, you up there," she yelled, "stop dropping berries. Animals live down here you know. You should be more careful."

Nearby, Crocodile was basking in the warm sun. Plonk, splash, plop. Plonk, splash, plop. A huge pile of nuts rained down on to the tip of his long nose.

"Ouch," snapped Crocodile. "That really hurt. Hey, you up there," he bellowed," stop dropping nuts. If you do that again, I'll gobble you up."

Hidden in the bushes beside the river's edge, Jaguar was sleeping. "Aaaah-choooo. Aaaah-chooo." Jaguar woke up with a loud sneeze. Something was tickling her nose.

A beautiful red tail feather was tangled in her whiskers.

'Now where did that feather come from?' wondered Jaguar. 'It must have floated down from the tree-tops.'

As she lay there, Jaguar could hear Frog and Crocodile complaining loudly.

"I was woken up again today." croaked Frog. "Sticky berries landing all over me. I look like blackberry jam."

26

"What a nuisance," replied Crocodile. "Another pile of nuts just hit me on the nose. I don't know where they keep coming from."

"Excuse me," interrupted Jaguar, popping out from behind the bushes. "I couldn't help overhearing you both. I think I know who it might be."

"Who?" asked Frog and Crocodile.

"The animal who dropped this," replied Jaguar, holding out the feather.

"If we match this feather to the right animal, we can ask them to stop dropping their food down on us," said Frog.

"We must send a message up to the tree-tops," said Crocodile.

So Frog and Crocodile wrote a polite letter, asking the owner of the feather to kindly stop dropping food.

To the owner of the feather.
Please stop dropping your food. You are disturbing the animals who live below you on the forest floor.

Thank you,
from Frog and Crocodile.

Jaguar, who was better at climbing trees, took the letter and the feather and started to climb. Halfway up, she heard a strange, gurgling noise. It was Sloth snoring, asleep as usual.

"Wake up, lazy-bones," whispered Jaguar. "I have something to show you."

Sloth opened the letter and read it. "The feather's not mine," yawned Sloth. "I'm just shaggy fur. And I never eat berries. I only like leaves. But I know who it might be. There's a little bat up above among the branches. She's always chewing fruit."

"Well, I can't climb up that high!" sniffed Jaguar. "Will you take this letter for me?"

"Oh, alright," moaned Sloth. "I guess I haven't moved an inch today."

In the morning, Sloth woke up to hear a screeching macaw swooping by. Just then, a flash of colour shimmered amongst the leaves.

Macaw squawked. "That's my feather you're holding. It fell off the other day. What are you doing with it?"

"Ahhhh..." said Sloth, blinking at Macaw's bright red tail feathers. "So it's you we've been looking for."

Macaw snatched the letter in her big curly claw and read it silently. When she'd finished, she let out a long whistle.

So Sloth started to climb. She was terribly slow. By the time she reached Bat, it was nearly night.

Sloth gave the letter to Bat. "This feather's not mine," Bat squeaked. "This is a bird's feather. I know I look a bit like a bird but I'm not." Bat stroked her fluffy body. "Oh, how I'd love to have pretty feathers like a bird. But I can't help you now. I've just woken up and I need some breakfast," and she flapped off into the night.

Sloth was exhausted from all the climbing. She went to sleep exactly where she was hanging.

"I didn't know there were animals living down there," squawked Macaw. "It's so wet, dark and gloomy. As for all the mess, I'm dreadfully sorry. I'm always spilling my food, as I like to talk with my mouth full."

"Well, I think you should try and be more careful," said Sloth. "There are animals living below you on the forest floor. You wouldn't want them coming up here and dropping their food on you, would you? Can you imagine that huge crocodile swinging about up here with those white, sharp teeth?"

"Definitely not!" shrieked Macaw, trembling with fear. "Tell Frog and Crocodile I'll be very sensible from now on. I won't drop food on them ever again."

So Sloth climbed back down to the forest floor as fast as she could. Frog, Crocodile and Jaguar were waiting when she finally arrived back.

"What took you so long?" asked Crocodile. "You're such a slow climber. It's been nearly a week since you left."

"Did you find the animal who dropped the feather?" asked Jaguar.

"I certainly did," answered Sloth proudly. "It was a colourful macaw. She was really chatty and dreadfully sorry about splattering fruit and nuts down here. She didn't think anyone would want to live down below her, where it's all dark and steamy."

"I hope she said she would stop too?" croaked Frog.

"Oh yes," grinned Sloth. "All I had to say was, 'how would you like it if Crocodile swung around up here and dropped his food down on you?' She looked really scared and immediately promised to be more careful."

"Well done, Sloth," said Frog.

"But I can't climb trees," whispered Crocodile.

"I didn't tell her that," winked Sloth. "That's our secret!"

Puzzles

Follow me!

Can you work out where the macaw, crocodile and jaguar live? Follow the lines to find out!

macaw   crocodile   jaguar

forest floor   tree-tops   river

Close up!

We've zoomed in on these animals' bodies. Can you work out which animals you are looking at?

1

2

3

True or false quiz

Can you work out which animals are telling the truth? You can go to the page numbers listed to help you find out the answers.

1 When a baby snake hatches, it bites a hole in its egg with a special tooth. **Go to page 19.**

2 A bird-eating spider can be as big as a table. **Go to page 23.**

3 A mother crocodile carries her babies in her mouth. **Go to page 20.**

4 A howler monkey never makes a noise. **Go to page 5.**

Answers: 1 true, 2 false, 3 true, 4 false.

Index